# Contents

Answer keys are online at:
http://cambridge.org/funresources

Michela Capone

# Animals

eagle

spaceship

**1** Can you guess the animal and spell it?

k a n g a r o o

_ _ _

_ _ _ _ _

_ _ _ _

_ _ _ _ _

_ _ _ _ _ _ _ _

**2** Read and guess the pet.

This is a story about my pet. One day my mum and dad took me to the pet shop to buy a new pet. I chose the most colourful one in the shop and took it home.
I called it Ocean because it was blue, yellow and green.

One day I came home from school and my new pet wasn't in its nest. My mum said, 'I'm sorry, it flew away.' I was very sad!

Then one day I was sitting in the garden and Ocean flew around me and landed on

my hand. I was so happy.

What pet is it? .........................................

**3** Draw what the animal does.

| | |
|---|---|
| A swan swims. | A rabbit eats vegetables. |
| A tortoise smiles. | A kangaroo hops. |

**4** Find the animals.

| t | e | a | g | l | e | b | g | f | e |
|---|---|---|---|---|---|---|---|---|---|
| o | o | t | o | c | e | u | s | e | b |
| r | c | a | m | e | l | t | b | l | e |
| t | t | b | l | o | s | t | r | s | e |
| o | o | u | e | a | m | e | r | u | t |
| i | p | s | x | e | l | r | s | v | l |
| s | u | w | d | b | o | f | w | d | e |
| e | s | a | b | a | t | l | a | g | y |
| l | i | z | a | r | d | y | n | k | s |
| c | r | o | c | o | d | i | l | e | e |

~~bat~~
bee
beetle
butterfly
camel
crocodile
eagle
lizard
octopus
swan
tortoise

**5** Put two or three animals together and draw a new animal. What is the name of this new animal?

eagle   lizard   octopus   swan   tortoise   shark   cat
bat   bee   beetle   butterfly   camel   crocodile   dog

abc ✓

How do you spell the words?

 _ _ _ _ _ _ _

_ _ _ _ _ _ _

# Clothes

**1** Draw the clothes on the woman and complete the words.

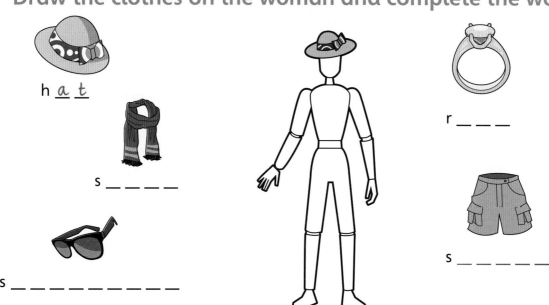

h _a_ _t_

s _ _ _ _ _

s _ _ _ _ _ _ _ _ _ _

r _ _ _ _

s _ _ _ _ _ _

**2** Put the clothes in the best wardrobe.

**Winter**

**Summer**

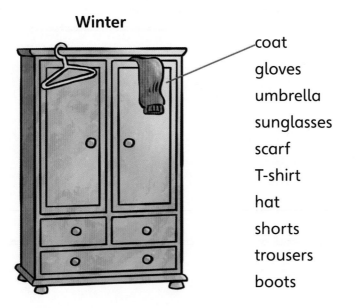

coat
gloves
umbrella
sunglasses
scarf
T-shirt
hat
shorts
trousers
boots

**3** Read about Sam. Write about you.

In Sam's winter wardrobe he has got a coat, gloves, a scarf, a hat, trousers and boots. What's in your summer wardrobe?

.................................................................................

.................................................................................

.................................................................................

**4** Put the letters in order. Then write the parts of the body.

h t a
.......hat.......

r c a f s
.....................

k s c o
.....................

n g i r
.....................

h _ _ _

n _ _ _

f _ _ _

f _ _ _ _ _

**5** Draw clothes for your mum and dad. Write a list of what they are wearing in your pictures.

............................
............................
............................
............................
............................
............................

............................
............................
............................
............................
............................
............................

abc ✓

How do you spell the word?

p _ _ _ _ _ _ _

# Colours

**1** **Complete the song with the colours. Look at the rainbow.**

1 .......... Red .......... and 2 .......................... and 3 .........................
and 4 ........................
5 ........................ and 6 ........................ and 7 ......................... .
I can sing a rainbow,
Sing a rainbow
Sing a rainbow too.

**Can you sing the song?**

1
2
3
4
5
6
7

**2** **Look at the picture. Read and colour and draw.**

1 The tree is brown.
2 The sun is yellow.
3 The chicken is orange.
4 The water is blue.
5 The boy with black hair is wearing a green T-shirt.
6 The girl is wearing a striped grey and pink dress.
7 The boy who is with the girl is wearing a spotted red shirt.
8 The big duck in the pond is grey.

**3** **The words in the boxes are wrong. Write the right colour.**

| red | white | silver | pink |
|---|---|---|---|
| yellow | | | |

| blue | green | brown | yellow |
|---|---|---|---|
| | | | |

**4** **Mix the colours. Draw and write the new colours.**

........black........ + ........white........ = ........grey........

.............................. + .............................. = ..............................

.............................. + .............................. = ..............................

.............................. + .............................. = ..............................

.............................. + .............................. + .............................. = ..............................

**5** *Fun at home* **Make or draw your animal mobile.**

Use different colours.

Ask and answer questions about your mobile.

What colour is the eagle?

*abc* ✓

How do you spell the word?

   t _ _ _ _ _ _ _

# Food and drink

**1** **Draw the words.**

chopsticks

spoon

bowl

plate

cup

fork

knife

glass

**2** **What do you use to eat and drink these?**

**1**
glass

**2**
...........................

**3**
...........................

**4**
...........................

**5**
...........................

**6**
...........................

**3** **What food is on the plates?**

pear, ...........................

onion, ...........................

...........................

...........................

# 4 Complete the words using the letters.

①

<u>c</u> <u>o</u> <u>f</u> <u>f</u> e

②

_ e _ _ n _ _ _ _

③

w _ _ _ _ r

| L | T | O | R | E | E | F | C | D | E | F | M | A | A |
|---|---|---|---|---|---|---|---|---|---|---|---|---|---|

| U | A | U | C | C | I | K | N | S | G | B | E | E | G | A |
|---|---|---|---|---|---|---|---|---|---|---|---|---|---|---|

④

_ h _ _ _ e _

⑤

_ _ r _ _ r

⑥

s _ _ s _ _ e

# 5 Fun at home Play the game with your family.

The rules:
1 On the question squares, ask your family a food question.
2 On the food pictures guess the food. If it is wrong, miss a turn.
  First to finish wins!

| START | Question Do you like sausages? | Food | Question What do you have for breakfast? | Food |
|---|---|---|---|---|
| | 1 | 2 | 3 | 4 |
| FINISH | Food | Question What's your favourite food and why? | Food | Question What's your favourite drink? |
| | 8 | 7 | 6 | 5 |

abc ✓

How do you spell the word?

l _ _ _ _

# Health

**1** **What's the matter? Match the words to the pictures.**

cough   temperature   headache   stomach-ache   earache   toothache   cold

**2** **Read the sentences and guess the words.**

1. The place you go when you are ill.                                   h <u>o</u> <u>s</u> <u>p</u> <u>i</u> <u>t</u> <u>a</u> <u>l</u>
2. The person who helps when you are ill.                               d _ _ _ _ _ _
3. The place where you buy medicine.                                    c _ _ _ _ _ _ _
4. The person who you go to when you have a toothache.   d _ _ _ _ _ _ _
5. What you take to feel better.                                       m _ _ _ _ _ _ _ _
6. The person who helps the doctor.                                    n _ _ _ _ _

**3** **Which word is different? Cross it out.**

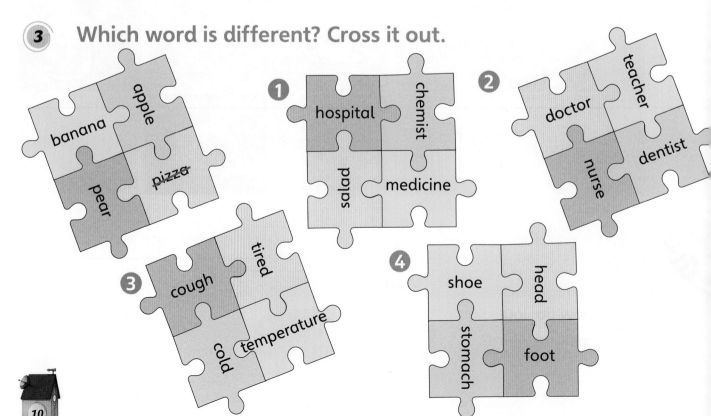

**4** **Which part of the body is it? Draw lines then draw the parts of the body.**

fingers

knees

toes

neck

arms

hands

shoulders

elbows

back

feet

**5** **Fun at home** **Write three questions about health. Ask your family. Who is the healthiest?**

| Question | Family person 1 | Family person 2 | Family person 3 | Family person 4 |
|---|---|---|---|---|
| Have you ever had a cough? | Yes, once | Yes, many times | Twice | No, I use medicine |
| 1 | | | | |
| 2 | | | | |
| 3 | | | | |

abc

How do you spell the words?

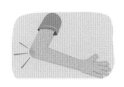 _ _ _ _

 _ _ _ _

# The home

**1** **Where are the rooms? Write the names of the rooms.**

**1** .....kitchen.....

**2** ........................

**3** ........................

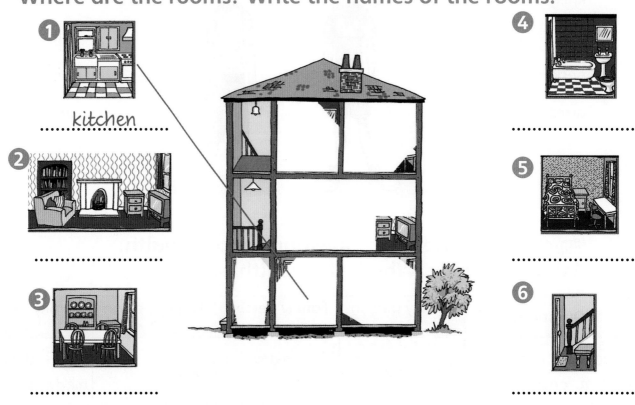

**4** ........................

**5** ........................

**6** ........................

**2** **Complete the crossword.**

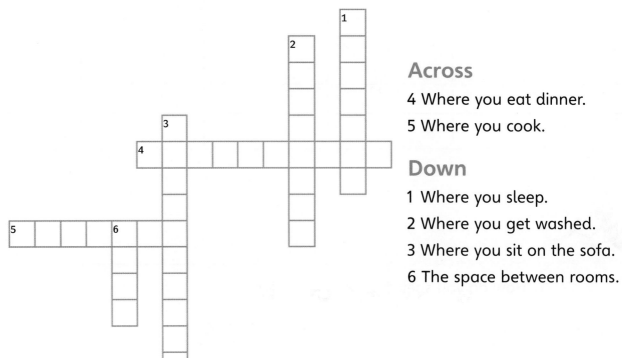

## Across

4 Where you eat dinner.

5 Where you cook.

## Down

1 Where you sleep.

2 Where you get washed.

3 Where you sit on the sofa.

6 The space between rooms.

12

**3** Look at the pictures. Can you guess the house objects?

c.omputer..........　　m......................　　l......................　　m......................

p....................　　c....................　　r....................

**4** **Fun at home** Choose a colour. Choose a number.
Answer the question.

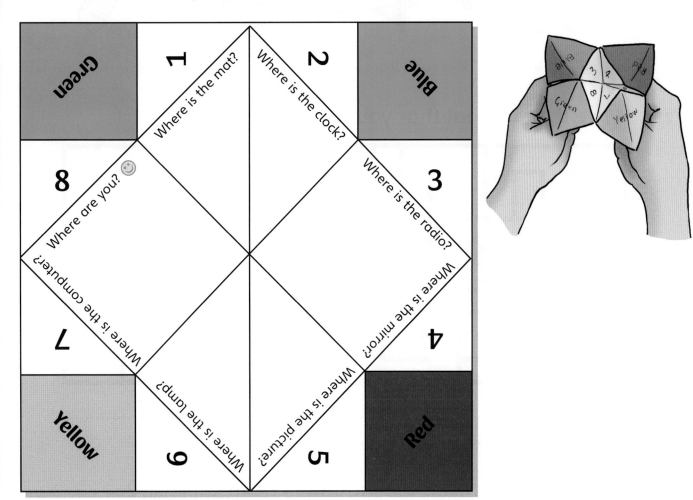

Green

1

Where is the mat?

Where is the clock?

2

Blue

8

Where are you? 😊

Where is the radio?

3

Where is the computer?

Where is the mirror?

Yellow

7

Where is the lamp?

Where is the picture?

4

9

5

Red

13

# Materials

**1** What are they made of?

> gold   wood   wool   paper   ~~silver~~   metal   glass   plastic

..........silver..........

.....................

.....................

.....................

.....................

.....................

.....................

.....................

**2** Write the material that you find in the maze.

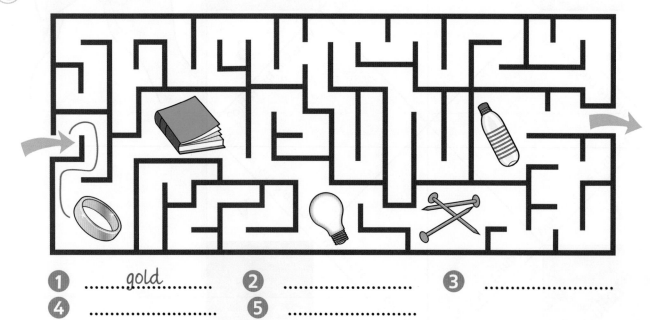

**1** ........gold..........   **2** .....................   **3** .....................

**4** .....................   **5** .....................

**3** Write sentences with the materials from exercise 2.

> book   light bulb   nails   bottle

**1** The ring is made of gold...

14

**4** **Draw lines between the letters to make materials.**

| 1 C | A | P | T | U | | |
|---|---|---|---|---|---|---|
| 1 P | S | I | E | R | | |
| 2 G | M | L | X | | | |
| 2 U | O | Y | D | | | |
| 3 F | W | R | D | | | |
| 3 C | A | Y | T | | | |
| 4 S | H | X | V | E | K | |
| 4 J | I | L | S | A | R | |
| 5 P | H | I | T | T | U | C |
| 5 C | L | A | S | A | I | B |

**1** ........*paper*..........

**2** ........................

**3** ........................

**4** ........................

**5** ........................

**5** **Fun at home** Put stickers on things in your living room and bedroom with the name of the material.

abc ✓

*wood*

How do you spell the word?

 p _ _ _ _ _ _

 s _ _ _ _ _

# Places and directions

**1** Write the names of the places.

...university......  a.........................  r.........................  c.........................

s.........................

m.........................  h.........................  p.........................

s.........................

**2** Write the correct number under the directions.

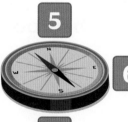

| South | Right | East | Straight on | West | Left | North |
|-------|-------|------|-------------|------|------|-------|
|       |       |      | 1           |      |      |       |

**3** Write the names of the places in the pictures.

 b u s   s t o p    _ _ _ _ _ _ _   _ _ _ _ _ _ _

 _ _ _ _ _ _ _   _ _ _ _ _ _ _

**4** **Look at the map of London. Complete the sentences.**

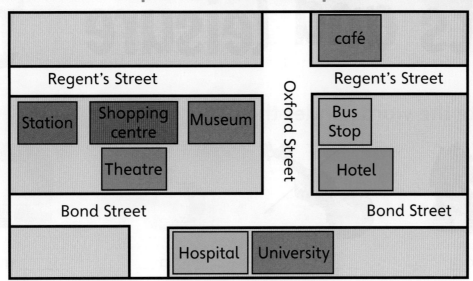

1 The theatre is ..........behind.......... the shopping centre.
2 The shopping centre is ........................ the station and the museum.
3 The hospital is ........................ the university.
4 The hotel is ........................ the bus stop.
5 The café is ........................ the bus stop.

**5** *Fun at home* **Draw your favourite place.**
**Describe the place to someone and say 'Where is it?'.**

I love to eat ice cream in this place. Where is it?

I like visiting this place so I can see animals from all over the world. Where is it?

abc ✓

How do you spell the words?

  _ _ _ _ _ _

  _ _ _ _ _ _

# Sports and leisure

**1** Complete the words under the pictures.

p l a y
c h e s s

_ _ a _
the
_ i o _ i _

_ _ a _
the
_ _ u _ _

_ _ a _
_ o _ _

_ _ o _ _ o a _ _ i _ _

_ _ i i _ _

_ _ a _
_ o _ _ e _ _ a _ _

**2** Match the verbs with the activities

| | |
|---|---|
| reading | a kite |
| joining | photos |
| collecting | on stage |
| acting | a club |
| going | comic books |
| taking | a quiz |
| doing | shopping |
| flying | football cards |

## 3 Read about John and answer True or False.

John is ten years old and he loves doing sports and activities in his free time. At the moment he plays football three times a week, on Monday, Wednesday and Friday from 4 until 6 p.m. He loves playing football because he likes being in a team. In his free time he collects football cards and puts them in a card book. When he was a child he played the violin, but he didn't enjoy it.

1 John is nine years old.                    .........................
2 He plays football three times a week.    .........................
3 He doesn't like being in a team.          .........................
4 He collects footballs.                     .........................

**What sports and activities do you like doing and why?**

.................................
.................................

## 4 Write the objects that are missing in the second box.

1 ......rucksack......    2 .........................    3 .........................
4 .........................    5 .........................

## 5 Fun at home Create a poster of your favourite sportsperson.

Collect pictures from magazines and write about his / her story.

| | |
|---|---|
| Name: | ......................... |
| Surname: | ......................... |
| Nationality: | ......................... |
| Sport: | ......................... |
| Age: | ......................... |
| Family: | ......................... |
| Description: | ......................... |
| Why you like him / her? | ......................... |

# School

**1** **What are these classroom objects?**

g l u e

_ _ n

_ c _ _ s _ _ _

_ _ p _ _ _ r _

_ l _ _

_ u _ _ s _ _ _

**2** **Where are the mice in the classroom? Draw and colour them.**

There is a pink mouse on the teacher's chair. There's a blue mouse in front of the flag. There's a green mouse between the middle desks. There's an orange mouse above the door. There's a big yellow mouse under the teacher's desk. There's a red mouse in the boy's rucksack. There's a purple mouse opposite the cupboard.

**3** **Do the word quiz. What subject is it?**

paint, draw, colour = .......... *art* ..........

song, singing, play = ..........................

the past, king, queen = ..........................

goal, playground, volleyball = ..........................

numbers, test, 4 + 1 = 5 = ..........................

English, dictionary, stories = ..........................

**4** **Put the words in the correct backpack.**

classroom, rubber, keyboard, English, student, flag, cupboard, glue, gym, history, project, playground, science, teachers, computer, maths, board, rucksack, shelf, geography, club, bookcase, art

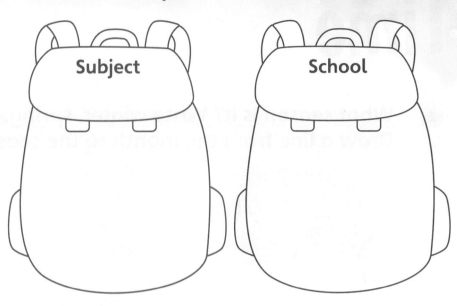

Subject

School

**5** **Fun at home** **Invent your favourite school timetable. Tell your family about it.**

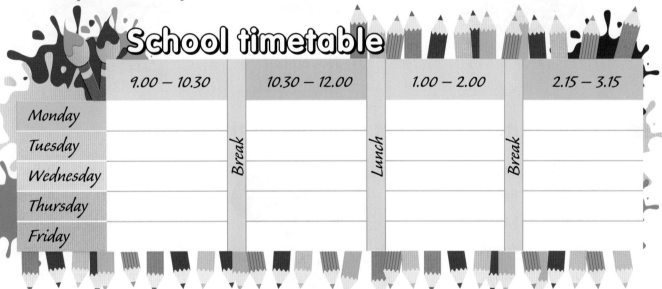

## School timetable

|  | 9.00 – 10.30 | | 10.30 – 12.00 | | 1.00 – 2.00 | | 2.15 – 3.15 |
|---|---|---|---|---|---|---|---|
| Monday | | Break | | Lunch | | Break | |
| Tuesday | | | | | | | |
| Wednesday | | | | | | | |
| Thursday | | | | | | | |
| Friday | | | | | | | |

What do you have on Monday at nine?

I have sport at nine on Monday.

abc ✓

How do you spell the word?

4+4=8
2 × 2
10÷2=5
6X2=12
10−7=3
4+1+7=12

h _ _ _ _ _ _ _

21

# Time

**1** What season is it? Write winter, spring, summer or autumn.
Draw a line from the month to the season.

winter

December
February
August
March
June
September
May
January
October
April
November
July

**2** Cross out the incorrect spellings of the months.

| | |
|---|---|
| January | ~~Jenuary~~ |
| February | Febbruari |
| Marc | March |
| April | Apryl |
| Mai | May |
| Giune | June |

| | |
|---|---|
| July | Juli |
| August | Aygost |
| September | Settembre |
| Octobe | October |
| November | Novembre |
| Dicember | December |

**3** Write the correct day.

| Day before | Today | Day after |
|---|---|---|
| Monday | Tuesday | Wednesday |
| | Sunday | |
| | Thursday | |
| | Saturday | |
| | Monday | |
| | Wednesday | |
| | Friday | |

**4** **Complete the sentences using the words below.**

> midnight   o'clock   Tonight   a.m.   p.m.   quarter   past   ~~Christmas~~   century

The 25th of December is ....*Christmas*..... .

00.00 is ......................... .

100 years is a ......................... .

In the morning we use ......................... .

7.45 is a ......................... to 8.

9.15 is a quarter ......................... 9.

It`s 5 ......................... .

In the afternoon we use ......................... .

......................... I'm going to the cinema.

**5** **Fun at home** **Write and say three dates of a friend or family member's birthdays or of an important holiday.**

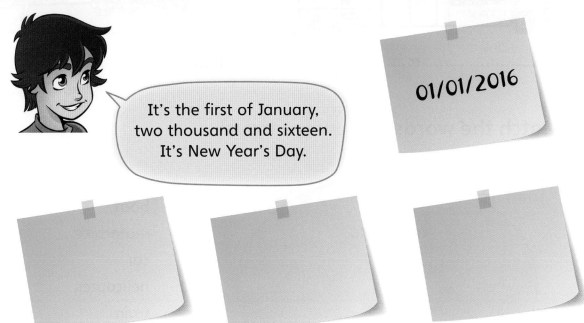

It's the first of January, two thousand and sixteen. It's New Year's Day.

01/01/2016

abc ✓

How do you spell the words?

y _ _ _ _ _ _ _

t _ _ _ _ _ _ _

23

# Transport

**1**  Write the different types of transport under the pictures.

t.<u>rain</u>................... l.<u>orry</u>...................

b.......................... r..........................

t......................... a.........................

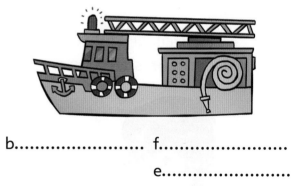

b.......................... f.........................

e.........................

**2**  Match the words to how we travel.

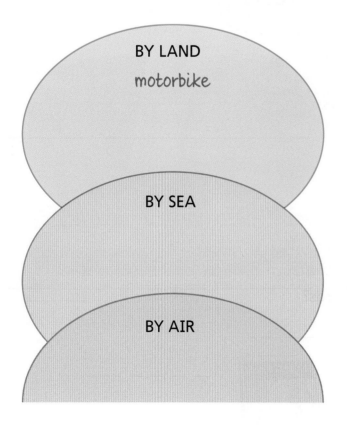

BY LAND

motorbike

BY SEA

BY AIR

boat

~~motorbike~~

car

helicopter

train

lorry

swim

bike

plane

taxi

bus

walk

**3** Look and read. Find the words in the car.

~~airport~~
passengers
traffic     railway station
ticket     timetable

**1** This is the place where you get a plane. ..........*airport*..........

**2** You need this to get onto any type of transport. You must pay for it.

.........................

**3** When there are a lot of cars on the road it creates this. ...........................

**4** This is the name for the people who use transport. ...........................

**5** You must check this before you travel. It tells you the time that your bus or train arrives. ...........................

**6** This is the place where you get the train. ...........................

**4** Circle the correct verb in the sentences.

I (go) / work to school.

He swims / drives a taxi.

I eat / fly a plane.

I ride / swim in the sea.

I run / sing in the park.

I go / ride my bike.

**5** Invent a new form of transport for the year 2080. Draw, colour and write about it.

This is my new form of transport. It's called a rocketaxi. It is a rocket that goes onto your back and flies you to wherever you want to go. You just tell it the address and it will take you there.

# Work

**1** ## Who uses these objects?

astronaut

businessman

police officer

fire fighter

cook

designer

mechanic

**2** ## What's the job? Complete the dominoes.

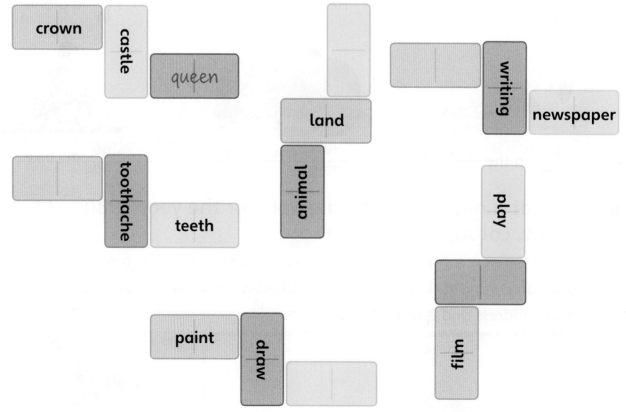

crown | castle | queen

land | animal

writing | newspaper

toothache | teeth

play

film

paint | draw

### 3 Look at the pictures and write the jobs.

c......oo......k          m..............c          p..............r          a..............s

s..............y          j..............t          d..............s

### 4 Fun at home Interview two people about their jobs. Create an information card for each person. Make questions.

Job: teacher

Where:

Uniform:

Like/dislike:

What time:

Hours:

Example question: What do you do?

..................................................

..................................................

..................................................

..................................................

..................................................

..................................................

..................................................

abc ✓

How do you spell the word?

f __ __ __ f __ __ __ __ __ __

# The world around us

**1** **Complete the planet quiz.**

**1** This planet is blue and green and we live on it. It's ......*Earth*........ .

**2** ........................ has the largest ring around it.

**3** We can see the ........................ from Earth at night.

**4** The ........................ makes the Earth warm.

**5** It is red, it is big, it is not far from Earth. It is ........................ .

**6** ........................ is the largest planet in the solar system.

**2** **Complete the weather table about Great Britain and Ireland.**

~~windy,~~ rainy, snowy, stormy, sunny, cloudy

| North Scotland | |
|----------------|--------|
| South Scotland | |
| Ireland | |
| North England | windy |
| Wales | |
| South England | |

**3** **Read what the weather's like in London, Great Britain and Ireland. What's the weather like in your country?**

Today in London the weather is sunny. In Scotland there is bad weather, there is a storm and it's snowing. In Ireland it will be sunny in the morning, but in the afternoon it will be cloudy.

.................................................................................................

.................................................................................................

.................................................................................................

**4** **Find the pictures and label them.**

d <u>e</u> <u>s</u> <u>e</u> <u>r</u> <u>t</u>            p _ _ _ _ _ _ _            j _ _ _ _ _ _

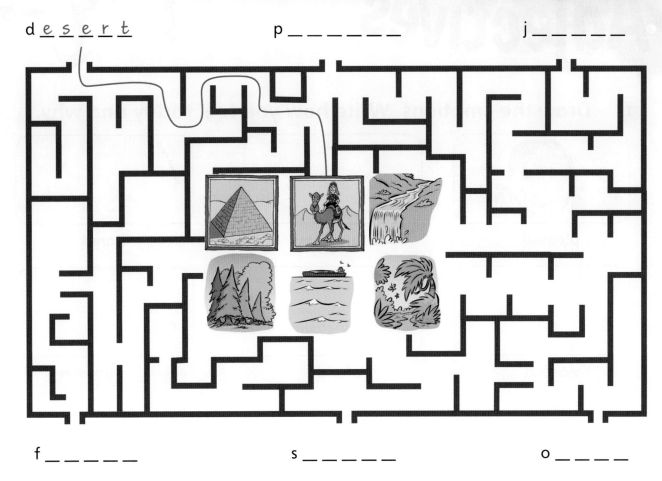

f _ _ _ _ _ _            s _ _ _ _ _ _            o _ _ _ _ _

**5** **Fun at home** **Make a poster about your favourite planet or star. Include information about it like this.**

Uranus is the seventh planet from the
sun and it is similar to Neptune. It is
the coldest planet in the solar system.

abc ✓

How do you spell the word?

e _ _ _ _ _ _ _

# Adjectives

**1** Draw the emotions. Write how you feel today and why.

| | | |
|---|---|---|
| pleased | unhappy | bored |
| worried | afraid | surprised |

Today I feel ...............................................................................
..................................................................................................

**2** Use these adjectives to describe the animals. You can use more than one.

~~furry~~ large ~~dangerous~~ friendly soft spotted thin small fat little

.......... The lion is furry and dangerous ..........

.................................................................

.................................................................

.................................................................

**3** Complete the table with the correct form of the adjectives.

| Adjectives | Comparative | Superlative |
|------------|-------------|-------------|
| good | better | the best |
| bad | | |
| | heavier | |
| | | the largest |
| | | the noisiest |
| dangerous | | |
| | lighter | |

**4** *Fun at home* Play the adjective game. Use the adjectives table to describe the words below.
The winner uses the most adjectives.

butterfly   octopus   swan   my mum   my dad   my bedroom
my living room   my English teacher   a bus

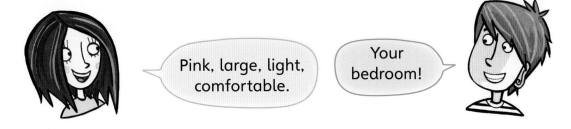

Pink, large, light, comfortable.

Your bedroom!

abc ✓

How do you spell the word?

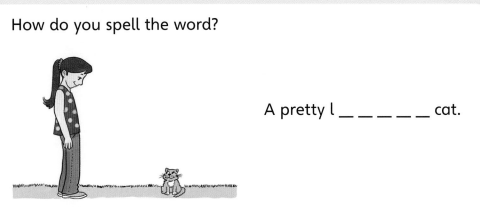

A pretty l _ _ _ _ _ cat.

The author would like to thank her friends and colleagues at the British Council, Naples for their support.

The author and publisher would like to thank the ELT professionals who reviewed the material at different stages of development: Lisa McNamara, Spain; Sarah Moore, Italy; Duygu Ozkankilic, Turkey; Jessica Smith, Italy.

Freelance Editorial Services by Trish Burrow.

Design and typeset by Wild Apple Design.

Cover design and header artwork by Chris Saunders (Astound).

Sound recordings by Ian Harker and dsound recording studios, London.

The authors and publishers acknowledge the following sources of copyright material and are grateful for the permissions granted. While every effort has been made, it has not always been possible to identify the sources of all the material used, or to trace all copyright holders. If any omissions are brought to our notice, we will be happy to include the appropriate acknowledgements on reprinting and in the next update to the digital edition, as applicable.

The publishers are grateful to the following for permission to reproduce copyright photographs and material

Key: L = Left, C = Centre, R = Right, T = Top, B = Below, B/G = Background

David Banks pp. 20(B), 21(B), 22(T), 25(B), 28(T); Adrian Bijoo (Advocate Art) pp.15; Bridget Dowty (Graham-Cameron Illustration) pp. p5(C), 7(C) (animal mobile), 8(B), 9(T), 9(C), 13(B); Andrew Elkerton (Sylvie Poggio Artists Agency) pp. 2, 3; Pablo Gallego pp. 4(B), 11(T), 19(M), 20(C), 23; John Haslam pp. 4(T), 5(T) (hat, scarf, sock, ring), 14, 17 (BR); Nigel Kitching pp. p4(M), 8(C), 10(T), 24(T); Nina de Polonia pp.7(CR), 21(CR), 31(C); Anthony Rule pp. 17, 19(T); Pip Sampson pp. 12, 16(B) 29(T); David Sones (Sylvie Poggio Artists Agency) pp. 2(eagle), 3(chicken), 5(B), 6(C), 9(B), 11(B), 16(C), 18(T), 25(C), 27(B), 29(B), 30(B); Tatiano Viana pp. 27(T); Matt Ward (Beehive Illustration): pp. 13(T), 16(B), 20(T), 22(C), 26(T), 29(T last 4); Sue Woollatt (Graham-Cameron Illustration) pp. 28(C), 29(C), 30(T), 31(B).